Poems and Paintings of the Malvern Hills

Poems and Paintings of the Malvern Hills

edited by Jonathan Lumby

Logaston Press

LOGASTON PRESS
Little Logaston Woonton Almeley
Herefordshire HR3 6QH
www.logastonpress.co.uk

First published by Logaston Press 2014
Selection and introductory matter © Jonathan Lumby 2014

ISBN 978 1 906663 84 1

Typeset by Logaston Press
and printed and bound in Poland by www.lfbookservices.co.uk

THE MALVERN HILLS separate *Herefordshire* from *Worcestershire*, and are about ten miles in length. Their direction is North and South. They consist of many sugar-loaf Hills, the summits of which command an extensive prospect, including parts of *Monmouthshire*, *Herefordshire*, *Radnorshire*, *Brecknockshire*, *Shropshire*, *Worcestershire*, and *Gloucestershire*. There is a spring rising in the side of one of the Hills, possessed of some medical properties, which, together with the purity of the air and the surrounding scenery, renders it a place of fashionable resort in the summer months.

Joseph Cottle, 1798

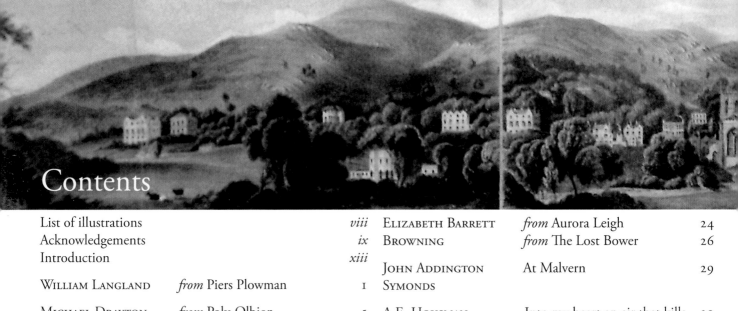

Contents

List of illustrations

Acknowledgements

This book has been enhanced by many who have shared enthusiasm for the Malverns and passion for poetry and painting. Philip Weaver of Ledbury, historian and painter, and Sue Locke of King's Caple, artist and anthologist, have encouraged me. Poet Margot Miller, together with Sue, suggested a local collection of poems. Heather Whatley, Chairman of the Friends of the Dame Laura Knight Society (Colwall and Malvern branch), showed me Laura's paintings. Always generous, Pat Welch, of White Leaved Oak, funded our plan to include some of them here. By good luck too I visited an exhibition in Ledbury of the works of Gilly Hancock; she has generously allowed us to include some of her paintings of the Malverns.

Pat Palmer of Malvern kindly photographed the picture of the hills which hangs in the office of the Malvern Hills Conservators – the picture on our Contents page. Roy Palmer, folklorist and editor of folk songs, introduced me to a poem – that by James Bisset; while Margaret Morse of White Leaved Oak introduced me to a poet – Jane Amherst, a writer and painter, who loves the hills. The Friends of the Dymock Poets focussed my interests; their Chairman Jeff Cooper, grandson of Lascelles Abercrombie, I count as a friend. Alan Bailey of Clitheroe, who attunes my ear to poetry, kindly commented on drafts of this book.

These contacts shaped what is before you.

Jonathan Lumby

STOW ON THE WOLD   CIRENCESTER   TETBURY   BATH   BRISTOL   CLIFTON

BOURTON ON WATER   STROUD   STONEHOUSE   BERKELEY   ORANGE COURT

CHELTENHAM   GLOUCESTER

BREDON HILLS

TEWKESBURY

LITTLE MALVERN

MALVERN WELLS

UPTON ON SEVERN

HANLEY CASTLE

COLLEGE

ASSEMBLY
ROOMS

PRIORY CHURCH

MALVERN:— VIEW FROM THE W

BRISTOL CHANNEL   NEWPORT   PONTYPOOL   MERTHYR TYDVIL   BRECON BEACONS

CHEPSTOW   PORTSKEWET   USK   BLAENAVON   CRICKHOWEL

FOREST OF DEAN   TINTERN   ABERGAVENNY   LLANTHONY ABBEY

DEAN   RAGLAN CASTLE   PONTRILAS   HEREFORD

MONMOUTH

GOODRICH CASTLE AND COURT   STOKE EDITH

ROSS

CAMP HILL

EASTNOR CASTLE   LEDBURY

COLWALL

BEACON

...STERSHIRE BEACON LOOKING SOUTH

'View of the Herefordshire Beacon, or British Camp, near Malvern', J.M.W. Turner

Introduction

I have collected these poems of the hills little by little, as one collects pearls. I value their beauty. Each poem has insight, wisdom, historical value or sheer elegance. Brought together, does each not resonate with the others?

You may enjoy this book of poems as a companion when you walk on the Malvern Hills. The poems celebrate Worcestershire Beacon, British Camp, The Gullet, Ragged Stone and Chase End, or they were written in or about places you can pick out from the heights – Little Malvern, the Chase, Eastnor, Ryton, Bredon Hill and May Hill. Also included are two townships hidden by hillocks, Ledbury and Dymock, the parish lands of which you can easily see.

'There is no more English spot in all England, and few more beautiful,' Bernard Levin wrote, having been in Malvern for its Festival. An agnostic himself, he continued, 'The view from my bedroom window was so extensive and spectacular that I was disappointed not to find Satan at my elbow promising me everything I could see if I would only fall down and worship him.'

I too gaze daily, amazed. On one day a valley-mist is pierced by church spires, on another the Cotswold escarpment under a blue sky looks clear and close.

Early in the 1800s Joseph Cottle, friend of Coleridge, climbed before dawn through cloud to the British Camp. The sky clears: '*Now on the Beacon's towering head I stand! / The radiant sun just peeps o'er yonder hill / In silent grandeur, whilst the neighbouring land, / Like ocean, drinks the splendour of the morn – / One mass of glory.'* Then: *'The goodly view makes my eye swim with rapture, and my heart/ Feels extasy . . .'* Still eyes swim; still tears fall. Two centuries apart, we and Joseph Cottle (though spelling it differently) can share one ecstasy.

My cottage sits high on Hollybed Common, where two centuries ago Welshmen drove herds through the hills. The drunkard father of poor Marian Erle in Elizabeth Barrett Browning's *Aurora Leigh* joined the drovers, and the squatters' cottage of the Erles, *'on a ledge of Malvern Hill / To eastward,'* was much as mine is. When drovers crested the pass at Hollybush they could peer at 'the coloured counties', the River Severn and Upton, the Vale of Evesham, Bredon's hill and Tewkesbury's tower towards which they headed.

☙

W.H. Auden, once a schoolmaster in Colwall (the boys called him 'Wizzy'), climbed to the hilltops: *'Here on the cropped grass of the narrow ridge I stand, / . . . Aloof as an admiral on the old rocks, / England below me: / Eastward across the Midland plains / An express is leaving for a sailor's country; / Westward is Wales . . .'* Auden described accurately. You know that the great poet stood where you, perhaps, are now standing.

Westward towards Wales a wide view unfolds, rumpled by hillocks and woods and lesser ridges. There Elizabeth Barrett Browning's brilliance flowered at Hope End, her family's home. Later, when she was in Italy, she described the landscape of her youth, the bumpiness of it – her word 'dimplement' makes me smile – *the ground's most gentle dimplement, / (As if God's finger touched but did not press/In making England!) such an up and down / Of verdure,– nothing too much up or down, / A ripple of land; such little hills, the sky / Can stoop to tenderly, and the wheatfields climb . . .'*

The eight-mile ridge of the Malverns lifts and lilts. Is its form like that of a dancer? Or like a musical air? Lascelles Abercrombie walked beside the Malverns homeward to Ryton: *'The Malvern Hills were with me all the way, / Singing loveliest visible melodies.'*

Here Edward Elgar said that he plucked his melodies from the very air: 'There is music in the air, music all around us, the world is full of it and you simply take as much of it as you require.' Ivor Gurney, another composer and one of our poets, in *Larches* described his art mystically as *'a saying of what the hill leaves unexprest'*.

Do you seek a good companion for your hike on the Malverns?

Wilfrid Gibson persuaded Geraldine to climb with him in icy weather to the Malverns' peak. In *Worcester Beacon*'s second stanza Gibson's short lines and silences are the gasps of those toiling uphill and of those whom love makes breathless. Perhaps Wilfrid and Geraldine would prefer to climb alone!

John Drinkwater and his companions however would welcome you if you *'bring lusty laughter . . . eager thought and speech that's keen'*. Or you may care to join Robert Frost and Edward Thomas, two superlative poets, as they tramp through Castlemorton Common, skirt the Reservoir, climb to British Camp and then, *'one another's guide'*, are *'groping down a Malvern side.'*

Poems show that these hills, gentle and harmonious, have evoked stupendous thoughts. Many a person walks abroad to ponder.

'*On a May morwenynge on Malverne Hilles*' when '*softe was the sunne*', in the mid 1300s, William Langland lay down '*under a brode banke by a bornes side.*' Will's rest by a stream was probably in Colwall. He '*slumbred in a slepying*'. A dream granted to him took Will over three hundred pages to expound in the winsome and witty poem, *The Vision of Piers Plowman*. Will exposed failings of the clergy, church and higher society, told of the whole '*fair feeld ful of folk*', and mused on love, generosity and true religion. The language of *The Vision* is the West Midlands form of English. This Malvern poem is a morning star of our nation's literature, quoted already in 1381 by John Ball, leader of the poor men of Essex in the Peasants' Revolt, and printed first in 1550 by Robert Crowley, later Archdeacon of Hereford, who admired *The Vision* as a forerunner of the Reformation and harbinger of social justice.

Another deep-thinking walker was Joseph Cottle. *Malvern Hills: a poem* is a thousand lines in length. The poet rejoices in the loveliness of the hills, and, as counterpoint, deplores 'Commerce' – the new capitalism – and proposes to alleviate the plight of the poor. He explained in a preface that '*these reflections were occasioned in some measure by visiting a poor family residing in a wretched hovel on the Herefordshire side of the Malvern Hills, and near the road at the bottom of the Herefordshire Beacon*'. He tells of the family's hunger – '*six small and half-starved children*' – and overcrowding. Sadly, an anthology does not allow for discursive pleading in poetic form. I can but report that the Malvern Hills evoked radicalism in William Langland and in Joseph Cottle, in Elizabeth Barrett Browning and in W.H. Auden. Here walking and talking have engaged with tragedy and with beauty, vision has gleamed with the visionary, and poets have wondered how we may treat each other more graciously.

❦

Melancholy struck some when parted from the Malverns. F.W. Harvey, caught in the hell of the trenches of Flanders, lamented: '*I'm homesick for my hills again – / My hills again!*' Elsewhere on the front his friend Ivor Gurney yearned for *'the up and down highway where go / Earth's pilgrims to wonder where Malvern upheaves / That blue emerald splendour under clouds of snow.'* The Malverns too may have been *'the blue remembered hills'* of A.E. Housman, and their surroundings his *'land of lost content'*, for Housman was reared in Bromsgrove.

❧

Ledbury was John Masefield's childhood home; from there he went to sea. Masefield's poems about his homeland lurch with his distinctive rhythms. *The West Wind* could be an anthem for Herefordshire, for *'the fine land, the west land, the land where I belong'*. In *Tewkesbury Road*, the road that crosses the Malverns at Hollybush, Masefield celebrates a landscape where *'the blessed green comely meadows seem all a-ripple with mirth'*.

Poets gathered in 1914 on the fringes of Dymock, in the hamlets of Ledington, Greenway and Ryton. Of them we have mentioned Lascelles Abercrombie, John Drinkwater, Wilfrid Gibson, Robert Frost and Edward Thomas. Should we be naming all poets from the western side of the Malverns, we would add John Masefield, W.H. Auden and Elizabeth Barrett Browning. The Malverns have repeatedly attracted to their foothills, and here nurtured, exceptional poetic talent. Today in different ways the Friends of the Dymock Poets, the John Masefield Society, the Autumn in Malvern Festival and the Ledbury Poetry Festival conserve, express and renew this poetic tradition.

❧

I have placed the poems in chronological order. William Langland of the 1300s starts the procession; Jane Amherst, our contemporary, ends it.

Jonathan Lumby

'September on Perseverance Hill', Gilly Hancock; Piers Plowman manuscript

In a Somer Seson, Whan Softe was the Sonne ...

In these opening lines Will enters a visionary state 'on a May morning on Malvern Hills'. This wonder may have happened beside a brook in the south-east part of the parish of Colwall. Herefordshire Beacon, topped by a keep, would be a 'tower on a toft' and from Colwall would be 'as high as the sun'. People in the 'fair field full of folk' begin to be described, each with his 'liflode' – his chosen way of life or livelihood. The poem thus gives us a glimpse of mediaeval society.

In a somer seson, whan softe was the sonne,	*sun*
I shoop me into shroudes as I a sheep were,	*I dressed myself in garments as though I were a sheep*
In habite as an heremite unholy of werkes,	
Wente wide in this world wondres to here.	*hear*
Ac on a May morwenynge on Malverne Hilles	*But; morning*
Me bifel a ferly, of Fairye me thoghte.	*I experienced a wonder, come from Fairy-power*
I was wery [of]wandred and wente me to reste	*I was weary, lost, and sought rest*
Under a brood bank by a bournes syde;	*stream (burn)*
And as I lay and lenede and loked on the watres,	*leaned down*
I slombred into a slepyng, it sweyed so murye.	*(the stream) sounded so sweet*
Thanne gan [me] to meten a merveillous swevene –	*to dream a wonderful vision*
That I was in a wildernesse, wiste I nevere where.	
As I biheeld into the eest an heigh to the sonne,	*east; high*
I seigh a tour on a toft trieliche ymaked,	*I saw a tower on a hillock, stylishly made*
A deep dale bynethe, a dongeon therinne,	*fortress*
With depe diches and derke and dredfulle of sighte.	*dark*
A fair feeld ful of folk fond I ther bitwene –	*field; found*
Of alle manere of men, the meene and the riche,	
Werchynge and wandrynge as the world asketh.	*working themselves*

I

Somme putten hem to the plough, pleiden ful selde,   *played (holidayed); seldom*
In settynge and sowynge swonken ful harde,   *planting; toiled*
And wonnen that thise wastours with glotonye destruyeth.   *gained what*
And somme putten hem to pride, apparailed hem therafter,
In contenaunce of clothynge comen disgised.   *showy clothing*
In preieres and penaunce putten hem manye,   *prayers*
Al for the love of Oure Lord lyveden ful streyte   *lived very strictly*
In hope to have heveneriche blisse –   *the bliss of heaven's kingdom*
As ancres and heremites that holden hem in hire selles,   *anchorites; cells*
Coveiten noght in contree to cairen aboute   *don't want to wander around the country*
For no likerous liflode hire likame to plese.   *luxurious way of life; their bodies*
And somme chosen chaffare; they cheveden the bettre –   *commerce (trade); succeeded*
As it semeth to oure sight that swiche men thryveth;
And somme murthes to make as mynstralles konne,   *entertain; know how*
And geten gold with hire glee – synnelees, I leeve.   *singing; innocently, I believe*

2

William Langland
from *Piers Plowman:*
The Prologue lines 1-34

'Harvest', Dame Laura Knight

Malverne, King of Hills

Whilst *Malverne* (king of Hills) fair *Severne* overlooks
(Attended on in state with tributary Brooks)
And how the fertile fields of *Hereford* do lie,
And from his many heads, with many an amorous eye
Beholds his goodly site, how towards the pleasant rise,
Abounding in excess, the Vale of *Eusham* lies,
The Mountains every way about him that do stand,
Of whom he's daily seen, and seeing doth command;
On tiptoes set aloft, this proudly uttereth he:
   Olympus, fair'st of Hills, that Heaven art said to be,
I not envy thy state, nor less myself do make;
Nor to possess thy name, mine own would I forsake:
Nor would I, as thou dost, ambitiously aspire
To thrust my forkéd top into th'etherial fire.
For, didst thou taste the sweets that on my face do breathe,
Above thou wouldst not seek what I enjoy beneath:
Besides, the sundry soils I everywhere survey,
Make me, if better not, thy equal every way.

Michael Drayton
from *Poly-Olbion* (1622)

*Drayton personifies Malvern as a king who overlooks fertile fields. Malvern boasts to Mount
Olympus that his own delights are equal to those around the abode of the gods.*

'The British Camp and Herefordshire Beacon', H.H. Lines

On spacious airy downs and gentle hills

On spacious airy downs and gentle hills,
With grass and thyme o'erspread, and clover wild,
Where smiling Phoebus tempers ev'ry breeze,
The fairest flocks rejoice! ... Wide airy downs
Are Health's gay walks to shepherd and to sheep.

                  ... Such ... the leas
And ruddy tilth which spiry Ross beholds,
From a green hiloc, o'er her lofty elms;
And Lemster's brooky tract, and airy Croft;
And such Harleian Eywood's swelling turf,
Wav'd as the billows of a rolling sea;
And Shobden, for its lofty terrace fam'd,
Which from a mountain's ridge, elate o'er woods,
And girt with all Siluria, sees around
Regions on regions blended in the clouds.
Pleasant Siluria, land of various views,
Hills, rivers, woods, and lawns, and purple groves
Pomaceous, mingled with the curling growth

Of tendril hops, that flaunt upon their poles,
More airy wild than vines along the sides
Of treacherous Falernum.

... Plough not such pasture; deep in spongy grass
The oldest carpet is the warmest lair,
And soundest; in new herbage coughs are heard.
  Nor love too frequent shelter: such as decks
The vale of Severn, Nature's garden wide,
By the blue steeps of distant Malvern wall'd,
Solemnly vast. The trees of various shade,
Scene behind scene, with fair delusive pomp
Enrich the prospect, but they rob the lawns.
Nor prickly brambles, white with woolly theft,
Should tuft thy fields. Applaud not the remiss
Dimetians*, who along their mossy dales
Consume, like grasshoppers, the summer hour;
While round them stubborn thorns and furze increase,
And creeping briars.

John Dyer
from *The Fleece*, Book I (1770)

* Dimetia, Carmarthenshire in south Wales
Dyer refers amusingly to the idleness of the natives of his own county.
Eywood is the home of a branch of the Harleys, the family of the Earl of Oxford.
Siluria is Herefordshire and the borderlands of Monmouth and Breconshire, anciently the land of the Silurii.
'Pomaceous' is the adjective from apple.

'Meadows at Colwall', Gilly Hancock

6

Gilly

Through Ledbury, at decline of day

... Through LEDBURY, at decline of day,
The wheels that bore us, roll'd away,
To cross the MALVERN HILLS. 'Twas night;
Alternate met the weary sight
Each steep, dark, undulating brow,
And WORC'STER'S gloomy vale below:
Gloomy no more, when eastward sprung
The light that gladdens heart and tongue;
When morn glanc'd o'er the shepherd's bed,
And cast her tints of lovely red
Wide o'er the vast expanding scene,
And mix'd her hues with mountain green;
Then, gazing from a height so fair,
Through miles of unpolluted air,
Where cultivation triumphs wide,
O'er boundless views on every side,
Thick planted towns, where toils ne'er cease,
And far-spread silent village peace,
As each succeeding pleasure came,
The heart acknowledg'd MALVERN'S fame.

Boast MALVERN, that thy springs revive
The drooping patient, scarce alive;
Where, as he gathers strength to toil,
Not e'en thy heights his spirit foil,
But nerve him on to bless, t'inhale,

And triumph in the morning gale;
Or noon's transcendent glories give
The vigorous touch that bids him live.
Perhaps e'en now he stops to breathe,
Surveying the expanse beneath?
Now climbs again, where keen winds blow,
And holds his beaver to his brow;
Waves to the *Wrecken* his white hand,
And, borrowing Fancy's magic wand,
Skims over WORC'STER'S spires away,
Where sprung the blush of rising day;
And eyes, with joy, sweet *Hagley Groves,*
That taste reveres and virtue loves;
And stretch'd upon thy utmost ridge,
Marks Severn's course, and UPTON-bridge,
That leads to home, to friends, or wife,
And all thy sweets, domestic life;
He drops the tear, his bosom glows,
That consecrated *Avon* flows
Down the blue distant vale, to yield
Its stores by TEWKESBURY'S deadly field,
And feels whatever can inspire,
From history's page or poet's fire.

Robert Bloomfield
from *The Banks of Wye* (1811)

'Church Lane, Ledbury', Gilly Hancock

At Malvern

I shall behold far off thy towering crest,
Proud mountain! from thy heights as slow I stray
Down through the distant vale my homeward way,
I shall behold upon thy rugged breast
The parting sun sit smiling: me the while
Escaped the crowd, thoughts full of heaviness
May visit, as life's bitter losses press
Hard on my bosom; but I shall beguile
The thing I am, and think that even as thou
Dost lift in the pale beam thy forehead high,
Proud mountain! whilst the scattered vapours fly
Unheeded round thy breast, so, with calm brow,
The shades of sorrow I may meet, and wear
The smile unchanged of peace, though pressed by care!

William Lisle Bowles
(July 17th 1793)

'On Top of Pinnacle Hill', Gilly Hancock

Malvern Hills

Joseph Cottle dedicated his long poem to his friend Robert Southey. In Malvern Hills *he expresses a radical social vision like that espoused by William Wordsworth and Samuel Taylor Coleridge, whose* Lyrical Ballads *Cottle was then publishing. Cottle challenges a society which allows wealth to coexist with the wretchedness of the poor. In a preface he writes:*

These reflections were occasioned in some measure by visiting a poor family residing in a wretched hovel on the Herefordshire side of the Malvern Hills, and near the road at the bottom of the Herefordshire Beacon. The family consists of a Husband, Wife, six small and half-starved Children, together with an aged Grandmother. The Husband is a Labourer, and in the best season of the year, earns from seven to ten shillings a week. It is no uncommon thing for such Families to kill one Pig in the year, and by partaking of it on particular days only, to make it last the whole of the following year. This was exactly the case with the present family. As I entered the door the pot was boiling over a small wood fire, round which the six ragged but innocent looking children with the old Grandmother were seated watching it boil with a solicitude that made them silent. The Mother was busily engaged in mending a garment that had been mended a hundred times before. She appeared to be a woman of good natural sense, and spoke like one who had known what grief was …

Malvern Hills, by Joseph Cottle (1798)

The ascent at dawn on Whit-Monday

Alone, unnoticed, at this early hour,
While all around is silence, I will mount
The MALVERN HILLS. This is a holy-day,
And holy I will make it, leave the world,
Its toils, and cares, and commune with myself.

　　　　As up I climb, the freshness of the morn
Smells grateful, though no object meet my view.
Through the dark mists, which now with coming day
Struggle for mastery, the giant Hill
Casts not a shade. Now back I turn, to mark
The winding path, but all is grey and void;
On every side thick clouds; the spacious world
Lives but in memory! whilst forth I roam
A wandering, unlov'd, solitary thing …

… What countless sun-beams glisten as I pass!
How sweet the early fragrance, as the dew
Rises with morn's pure incense to the skies!
The mount is still before me, and my feet
Must tread the mazy circuit, rough and steep,
Ere I attain the summit, but the view,
Spacious and grand, shall well repay the toil.

The Beacon

Now on the BEACON's towering head I stand!
The radiant sun just peers o'er yonder hill
In silent grandeur, whilst the neighbouring land,
Like ocean, drinks the splendour of the morn –
One mass of glory. Now the last faint star
Withdraws his timid ray, and slow the moon
Sinks shadowy in the western hemisphere.
Beneath my feet, down the dark mountain's side.
The clouds are troubled! now dissolve they fast!
A fairy vision! whilst the early Lark
Up through their bosom mounts most merrily.

　　　　… How bright the scene!
Now the low cots appear, the distant hills.
The fertile plains, far stretch'd on every side;
Whilst all the vast variety of forms
In yonder sunny vale, tranquil and fair,
O'erpower my ravish'd senses. What a sweep
For mortal eye! Trees of an hundred years.
From this huge mount, look like some tender sprays
And mock the toil to separate; whilst flocks,
And scattered herds, so faintly meet my sight,

They seem not living things. The goodly view
Makes my eye swim with rapture, and my heart
Feel extasy …

Upton on Severn

… And now I mark where Upton's spires arise,
Whilst many stately trees, and many cots,
And villages o'erspread the country round;
And orchards, with their odoriferous breath,
That scent the air, and to the eye present
One sheet of blossoms. Lovely scene! my heart
Almost disclaims humanity's dull powers,
And thinks it were a task of easy sort
To glide an airy shape amid the sky,
Or through yon pleasant vallies; drinking more
Of heaveny extasy: ah fond deceit!

Malvern Chase

From Hills that in the distance die away
I turn to mark the Chace. Trees that just rise
Above the tufted fern, in one long line
Of tasteless order, and the bounds of earth

And partial barrenness, and mould'ring trunks
Clad in their russet dress, proclaim that man
With sacrilegious hand hath labour'd long
To tame its wild luxuriance, and destroy
The haunts of hermit innocence and peace.
In vain the eye enquires for that great track
Of forest, thickly strew'd with giant Elms,
That once adorn'd the circling plain beneath
Whose lofty tops, e'en, jealous, Malvern view'd
And felt himself less vast. No longer now,
The thick-entangled trees engender damps,
And secret vapours – pestilent and foul.
The fragrant orchard, and the waving corn
O'erspread the cultured ground, and life, and health,
And cheerfulness, pervade the spacious scene.
But not that thou art chang'd from wood to field
And fragrant orchard, not that thy rich corn
Enchants the gazer, and repays the toil
Of patient man, do I thy praises sing,
Not that they woods are levell'd, thy tall trees,
That dared the blast, and check'd e'en Malvern's pride,
But that the laws which rule the royal lands
Are now no more – foul curse of ages past!

15

'The Malvern Hills', Dame Laura Knight

The Severn

... Each moment brings some secret object forth!
Old Severn there his eager current rolls,
Urging his stately undiverted course,
Impatient to embrace his parent Flood.
And many pleasant streams that from these hills
Take their meandring way, now meet mine eye;
The sun-beams sparkle on their humble waves,
That, hid awhile by little hills or trees,
Seem lost, then reappear, and onward steal
Gladd'ning the villagers. ...

The Holy Well

                        And now I mark.
Beneath two lofty hills, and in the vale
Form'd by their steep descent, the Holy Well.
A plain stone dwelling, weather-worn and rude,
Stands singly by. There never sound is heard
But the bleak wind, that, howling from above.
Sweeps the bald mountain's side, and urging on
Its boisterous way, at length forgets its rage,
In dallying with the valley's scattered trees ...

Distant churches

        ... From this high spot,
How many spires and aged towers appear;
Clear, or by distance dimm'd. – Most sweet to think
That these are temples to the living God,
Rais'd by our pious fathers, who, beneath
Their ever changing shades, now rest in peace.

Little Malvern Priory

Just peeping from a woody covert near
The lesser Malvern stands. Sequester'd church!
The spot around thee speaks of quietness.

Down at the mountain's base thou long hast brav'd
With unmov'd front, the season's varying hour,
The vernal tempest and December storms;
Yet at this tranquil time most fair thou seem'st:
The aged oaks around and stately elms
In wild luxuriance spread their unshorn limbs;
And, true to friendship, ward each angry blast
That, howling through the valley, sweeps along

To thy dark battlements. Protected stand
Through many a coming year, thou humble Tower!
And may thy sylvan guardians flourish too,
The woodman pass them, and the tempest spare.

Bronsil Castle

A musing melancholy fills the mind
As we behold where Bransil turrets stood,
How are the days gone by! how chang'd the scene
Since, circled by a vast and rich domain,
Its towers arose, majestic, moated round,
And made to bear the rust of ages! now
The neighbouring shepherd scarce can point the place
Where once they stood! – Significant of Man!
Where are the countless generations past? ...

... Farewell, delicious spot! I now must leave you;
Now must return to breathe pollution's air;
To mix with men, envelop'd in the cares
Of life; to be envelop'd too; to hear
Their converse low, how best to meet with wealth,
And to preserve that end of life till death.

It must be so, yet I will love to think
On you, dear Mount! and ponder on the joys
This morn bestow'd, and say, pressing my heart,
Than to review with memory's musing eye
Your lofty summit, mark its subject vales,
Its many scatter'd spires, and hamlets small,
And hear the magic orisons of birds,
Breaking the silence with their melody;
Not sweeter to the nightly traveller's ear
Sounds the soft lute, while wandering by the side
Of some slow stream, when, not a whispering breeze
Awakes the groves, and not a murmur, rude,
Impedes the warbled notes – expiring slow;
While the clear moon resplendent shines aloft.
And casts her pale beam o'er the sleeping tide.

Joseph Cottle
from *Malvern Hills*
(extracts from the 1,000-line
poem, 1798)

The Essington Hotel

At Malvern Wells, where health bears the bell,
All visitors notice the famous hotel
By Essington kept, where you meet with good cheer
Good wines and good liquors, good ale and good beer.
Of damp beds and rough treatment no person's in danger,
Whilst civil attention is paid to each stranger.
Then honour the house if you please; if you call
The Essingtons cheerly will wait on you all
To serve you with zeal, and obey each behest.
They'll endeavour to please you by doing their best.

James Bisset
from the guestbook of Essington Hotel
(about 1825)

Samuel Essington built the Essington Hotel at Malvern Wells in 1820. James Bisset of Leamington stayed there soon after it opened. By 1830 Mary Essington, Samuel's widow, was in charge. The hotel received guests until the early 1990s. It was then converted into flats known as Essington House.

St Catherine of Ledbury

When human touch (as monkish books attest)
Nor was applied nor could be, Ledbury bells
Broke forth in concert flung adown the dells,
And upward, high as Malvern's cloudy crest;
Sweet tones, and caught by a noble Lady blest
To rapture! Mabel listened at the side
Of her loved mistress; soon the music died.
And Catherine said, Here I set up my rest.

Warned in a dream, the Wanderer long had sought
A home that by such miracle of sound
Must be revealed: she heard it now, or felt
The deep, deep joy of a confiding thought;
And there, a saintly Anchoress, she dwelt
Till she exchanged for heaven that happy ground.

William Wordsworth
(1835)

Wordsworth wrote this sonnet in Brinsop, Herefordshire. The Wordsworths often visited Mary's brother Tom Hutchinson, who first farmed at Hindwell Farm near Kington and later lived in Brinsop Court near Hereford. A legend tells that Catherine, a holy lady, with her maid Mabel, searched for an anchorhold where she might live in piety. She had received heavenly assurance that her place would reveal itself; bells in a tower would ring without the agency of bell-ringers.

Malvern Hills

Erewhile I saw ye faintly through far haze
Spread many miles above the fields of sea;
Now ye rise glorious, and my steps are free
To wander through your valleys' beaten ways,
And climb above, threading the rocky maze;
And trace this stream alive with shifting light,
With whose successive eddies silver-bright
Not without pleasant sound the moonbeam plays.
My dear, dear bride, two days had made thee mine,
Two days of waxing hope and waning fear,
When under the night-planet's lavish shine
We stood in joy, and blessed that rillet clear;
Such joy unwarning comes and quickly parts,
But lives deep-rooted in our heart of hearts.

Henry Alford
Sonnet XLIII
(March 12th 1835)

'Looking South Along the Ridge', Gilly Hancock

'Walking Towards the Camp', Gilly Hancock

The Armada (excerpt)

... From Eddystone to Berwick bounds, from Lynn to Milford Bay,
That time of slumber was as bright and busy as the day;
For swift to east and swift to west the ghastly war-flame spread,
High on St. Michael's Mount it shone: it shone on Beachy Head.
Far on the deep the Spaniard saw, along each southern shire,
Cape beyond cape, in endless range, those twinkling points of fire. ...

... And on, and on, without a pause, untired they bounded still:
All night from tower to tower they sprang; they sprang from hill to hill:
Till the proud Peak unfurled the flag o'er Darwin's rocky dales,
Till like volcanoes flared to heaven the stormy hills of Wales,
Till twelve fair counties saw the blaze on Malvern's lonely height,
Till streamed in crimson on the wind the Wrekin's crest of light,
Till broad and fierce the star came forth on Ely's stately fane,
And tower and hamlet rose in arms o'er all the boundless plain ...

Thomas Babington Macaulay
(1842)

This passage tells of the lighting of beacons to alert England's defences. The Armada set sail in May 1588. It was harassed down the Channel by English vessels, cooped in Flanders, then confused by eight fire-ships on 28th July. Turning north, the Armada was battered by terrible storms around Scotland and Ireland. Of its 136 ships, 82 were lost.

The ground's most gentle dimplement

From Book I

I learnt to love that England. Very oft,
Before the day was born, or otherwise
Through secret windings of the afternoons,
I threw my hunters off and plunged myself
Among the deep hills, as a hunted stag
Will take the waters, shivering with the fear
And passion of the course. And when at last
Escaped, – so many a green slope built on slope
Betwixt me and the enemy's house behind,
I dared to rest, or wander, in a rest
Made sweeter for the step upon the grass,
And view the ground's most gentle dimplement,
(As if God's finger touched, but did not press
In making England), such an up and down
Of verdure, – nothing too much up or down,
A ripple of land; such little hills, the sky
Can stoop to tenderly and the wheatfields climb;
Such nooks of valleys lined with orchises,
Fed full of noises by invisible streams;
And open pastures where you scarcely tell
White daisies from white dew, – at intervals

The mythic oaks and elm-trees standing out
Self-poised upon their prodigy of shade, –
I thought my father's land was worthy too
Of being my Shakespeare's.

From Book III

We talked. She told me all her story out,
Which I'll re-tell with fuller utterance,
As coloured and confirmed in after times
By others, and herself too. Marian Erle
Was born upon the ledge of Malvern Hill,
To eastward, in a hut built up at night,
To evade the landlord's eye, of mud and turf,
Still liable, if once he looked that way,
To being straight levelled, scattered by his foot,
Like any other anthill ...

                              ... So she said,
Her father earned his life by random jobs
Despised by steadier workmen – keeping swine

On commons, picking hops, or hurrying on
The harvest at wet seasons, or, at need,
Assisting the Welsh drovers, when a drove
Of startled horses plunged into the mist
Below the mountain-road, and sowed the wind
With wandering neighings. In between the gaps
Of such irregular work he drank and slept,
And cursed his wife because, the pence being out,
She could not buy more drink. At which she turned,
(The worm), and beat her baby in revenge
For her own broken heart. There's not a crime
But takes its proper change out still in crime,
If once rung on the counter of this world:
Let sinners look to it.

Elizabeth Barrett Browning
from *Aurora Leigh* (1856)

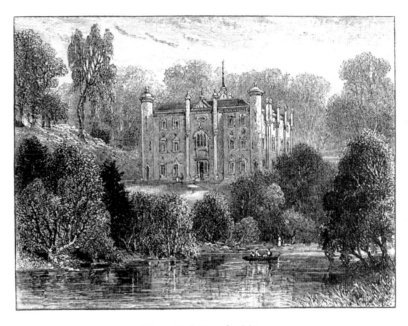

Hope End, Herefordshire

Elizabeth Barrett Browning described Aurora Leigh *as a 'novel in verse'. It is the life-story of a woman writer. Elizabeth sets these parts of the work around Hope End, where she had lived for 26 years.*

Green the land is

Green the land is where my daily
Steps in jocund childhood played,
Dimpled close with hill and valley,
Dappled very close with shade:
Summer-snow of apple-blossoms running up from glade to glade.

There is one hill I see nearer
In my vision of the rest;
And a little wood seems clearer
As it climbeth from the west,
Sideway from the tree-locked valley, to the airy upland crest.

Small the wood is, green with hazels,
And, completing the ascent,
Where the wind blows and sun dazzles,
Thrills in leafy tremblement,
Like a heart that after climbing beateth quickly through content.

Not a step the wood advances
O'er the open hill-top's bound;
There, in green arrest, the branches
See their image on the ground:
You may walk beneath them smiling, glad with sight and glad with sound.

For you hearken on your right hand,
How the birds do leap and call
In the greenwood, out of sight and
Out of reach and fear of all;
And the squirrels crack the filberts through their cheerful madrigal.

On your left, the sheep are cropping
The slant grass and daisies pale,
And five apple-trees stand dropping
Separate shadows toward the vale,
Over which, in choral silence, the hills look you their 'All hail!'

Far out, kindled by each other,
Shining hills on hills arise,
Close as brother leans to brother
When they press beneath the eyes
Of some father praying blessings from the gifts of paradise.

While beyond, above them mounted,
And above their woods alsò,
Malvern hills, for mountains counted
Not unduly, loom a-row –
Keepers of Piers Plowman's visions through the sunshine and the snow.

Elizabeth Barrett Browning
The Lost Bower, stanzas II to IX

At Malvern

The winds behind me in the thicket sigh,
The bees fly droning on laborious wing,
Pink cloudlets scarcely float across the sky,
September stillness broods o'er ev'rything.

Deep peace is in my soul: I seem to hear
Catullus murmuring 'Let us live and love;
Suns rise and set and fill the rolling year
Which bears us deathward, therefore let us love;

Pour forth the wine of kisses, let them flow,
And let us drink our fill before we die.'
Hush! in the thicket still the breezes blow;
Pink cloudlets sail across the azure sky;
The bees warp lazily on laden wing;
Beauty and stillness brood o'er ev'rything.

John Addington Symonds
(?1862)

'Sundown', Dame Laura Knight

'Into my heart an air that kills ...'

Into my heart an air that kills
  From yon far country blows:
What are those blue remembered hills,
  What spires, what farms are those?

That is the land of lost content,
  I see it shining plain,
The happy highways where I went
  And cannot come again.

A.E. Housman
A Shropshire Lad XL (1896)

In summertime on Bredon

In summertime on Bredon
    The bells they sound so clear;
Round both the shires they ring them
    In steeples far and near,
    A happy noise to hear.

Here of a Sunday morning
    My love and I would lie,
And see the coloured counties,
    And hear the larks so high
    About us in the sky.

The bells would ring to call her
    In valleys miles away:
"Come all to church, good people;
    Good people, come and pray."
    But here my love would stay.

And I would turn and answer
    Among the springing thyme,
"Oh, peal upon our wedding,
    And we will hear the chime,
    And come to church in time."

But when the snows at Christmas
    On Bredon top were strown,
My love rose up so early
    And stole out unbeknown
    And went to church alone.

They tolled the one bell only,
    Groom there was none to see,
The mourners followed after,
    And so to church went she,
    And would not wait for me.

The bells they sound on Bredon
    And still the steeples hum.
"Come all to church, good people," –
    Oh, noisy bells, be dumb;
    I hear you, I will come.

A.E. Housman
A Shropshire Lad XXI (1896)

Bredon is pronounced 'Breedon' (Housman's note)

Personal

Tramping at night in the cold and wet, I passed the lighted inn,
And an old tune, a sweet tune, was being played within.
It was full of the laugh of the leaves and the song the wind sings;
It brought the tears and the choked throat, and a catch to the heart-strings.

And it brought a bitter thought of the days that now were dead to me,
The merry days in the old home before I went to sea –
Days that were dead to me indeed. I bowed my head to the rain,
And I passed by the lighted inn to the lonely roads again.

John Masefield
(1902)

Tewkesbury Road

It is good to be out on the road, and going one knows not where,
  Going through meadow and village, one knows not whither nor why;
Through the grey light drift of the dust, in the keen cool rush of the air,
  Under the flying white clouds, and the broad blue lift of the sky;

And to halt at the chattering brook, in the tall green fern at the brink
  Where the harebell grows, and the gorse, and the foxgloves purple and white;
Where the shy-eyed delicate deer troop down to the pools to drink,
  When the stars are mellow and large at the coming on of the night.

O! to feel the warmth of the rain, and the homely smell of the earth,
  Is a tune for the blood to jig to, a joy past power of words;
And the blessed green comely meadows seem all a-ripple with mirth
  At the lilt of the shifting feet, and the dear wild cry of the birds.

John Masefield
(1902)

Masefield's early home was in Ledbury. His 'Tewkesbury Road' is that which runs through Eastnor, crosses the Malvern Hills at Hollybush and skirts Birtsmorton.

On Eastnor Knoll

Silent are the woods, and the dim green boughs are
Hushed in the twilight: yonder, in the path through
The apple orchard, is a tired plough-boy
Calling the cows home.

A bright white star blinks, the pale moon rounds, but
Still the red, lurid wreckage of the sunset
Smoulders in smoky fire, and burns on
The misty hill-tops.

Ghostly it grows, and darker, the burning
Fades into smoke, and now the gusty oaks are
A silent army of phantoms thronging
A land of shadows.

John Masefield
(1902)

Masefield slightly adapts the Sapphic, the unrhymed form and metre used by the Greek poetess of Lesbos.

'The Plough', Dame Laura Knight

On Malvern Hill

A wind is brushing down the clover,
  It sweeps the tossing branches bare,
Blowing the poising kestrel over
  The crumbling ramparts of the Caer.

It whirls the scattered leaves before us
  Along the dusty road to home,
Once it awakened into chorus
  The heart-strings in the ranks of Rome.

There by the gusty coppice border
  The shrilling trumpets broke the halt,
The Roman line, the Roman order,
  Swayed forwards to the blind assault.

Spearman and charioteer and bowman
  Charged and were scattered into spray,
Savage and taciturn the Roman
  Hewed upwards in the Roman way.

There – in the twilight – where the cattle
  Are lowing home across the fields,
The beaten warriors left the battle
  Dead on the clansmen's wicker shields.

The leaves whirl in the wind's riot
  Beneath the Beacon's jutting spur,
Quiet are clan and chief, and quiet
  Centurion and signifer.

John Masefield
(1902)

The West Wind

It's a warm wind, the west wind, full of birds' cries;
I never hear the west wind but tears are in my eyes.
For it comes from the west lands, the old brown hills.
And April's in the west wind, and daffodils.

It's a fine land, the west land, for hearts as tired as mine,
Apple orchards blossom there, and the air's like wine.
There is cool green grass there, where men may lie at rest,
And the thrushes are in song there, fluting from the nest.

"Will ye not come home, brother? ye have been long away,
It's April, and blossom time, and white is the may;
And bright is the sun, brother, and warm is the rain, –
Will ye not come home, brother, home to us again?

"The young corn is green, brother, where the rabbits run,
It's blue sky, and white clouds, and warm rain and sun.
It's song to a man's soul, brother, fire to a man's brain,
To hear the wild bees and see the merry spring again.

"Larks are singing in the west, brother, above the green wheat,
So will ye not come home, brother, and rest your tired feet?
I've a balm for bruised hearts, brother, sleep for aching eyes,"
Says the warm wind, the west wind, full of birds' cries.

It's the white road westwards is the road I must tread
To the green grass, the cool grass, and rest for heart and head,
To the violets and the warm hearts and the thrushes' song,
In the fine land, the west land, the land where I belong.

John Masefield
(1902)

Bredon

Bredon is a lonesome hill,
   It hasn't any brothers;
It stands within the Severn vale,
   Apart from all the others.

The Cotswold Hills go hand in hand.
   The Malverns touching shoulder;
But Bredon all alone does stand,
   More proud than they, and bolder.

Then it's on Bredon I will roam
   The livelong summer through;
For I've no brothers, I've no mate,
   And I be lonesome too!

Radclyffe Hall
(1913)

This and the following poems by Radclyffe Hall were originally published in Songs of Three Counties *and written to be set to music.*

The Hills

When I the hills of Malvern see,
There comes a sadness over me.

The reason why, I cannot tell,
Perhaps I love those hills too well.

But this I know, when I behold
Their springtime green, and autumn gold,

And see that year by year they bear
Such witness that God's earth is fair,

I'm happy for their beauty's sake,
And yet my heart begins to ache.

Radclyffe Hall
(1913)

The Malvern Hills

The Malvern Hills be green some days,
   And some days purple-blue,
There never was the like of them
   The whole of England through.

From Hanley straight into the Wells
   The road runs long and white,
And there the hills they meet your gaze
   Against the evening light.

Against the evening light they stand,
   So proud, and dark, and old,
The Raggedstone and Hollybush,
   And Worcester Beacon bold.

No matter where you chance to be,
   However far away,
You'll see the hills awaiting you
   At close of every day.

Oh! it's a lovely sight to see
   The twilight stealing down
Their steepish banks and little paths,
   Along to Malvern town.

And maybe on the Severn side,
   Hung low on Bredon's mound,
The big red harvest moon will rise,
   So lazy-like and round.

They talks a lot o' foreign parts,
   Them as has seen them do,
But give me Malvern Hills at dusk
   All green or purple-blue!

Radclyffe Hall
(1913)

'Changing Weather', Dame Laura Knight

Eastnor Churchyard

I be hopin' you remember,
Now the Spring has come again,
How we used to gather violets
By the little church at Eastnor,
For we were so happy then!

O my love, do you remember
Kisses that you took and gave?
There be violets now in plenty
By the little church at Eastnor,
But they're growing on your grave.

Radclyffe Hall
(1913)

The Meeting Place

I mind me of the hawthorn trees,
  With cuckoos flying near;
The hawthorn blossoms smelt so sweet,
  The cuckoo called so clear!

The hill was steep enough to climb.
  It seemed to touch the sky!
You saw two valleys from the top,
  The Severn and the Wye.

The Severn and the Wye you saw,
  And they were always green;
I think it was the prettiest sight
  That I have ever seen.

And there, so far above the town.
  With not a soul to see.
Whenever she could slip away
  My love would come to me!

I never smell the hawthorn bloom,
  Or hear the cuckoo sing,
But I am minded of my love,
  And Malvern Hills in Spring!

Radclyffe Hall
(1913)

The Road Not Taken

Two roads diverged in a yellow wood,
And sorry I could not travel both
And be one traveler, long I stood
And looked down one as far as I could
To where it bent in the undergrowth;

Then took the other, as just as fair,
And having perhaps the better claim,
Because it was grassy and wanted wear;
Though as for that the passing there
Had worn them really about the same,

And both that morning equally lay
In leaves no step had trodden black.
Oh, I kept the first for another day!
Yet knowing how way leads on to way,
I doubted if I should ever come back.

I shall be telling this with a sigh
Somewhere ages and ages hence:
Two roads diverged in a wood, and I –
I took the one less traveled by,
And that has made all the difference.

Robert Frost
(1916)

Whenever Robert Frost walked with Edward Thomas in Dymock Woods, Thomas vacillated between possible routes. Thomas was also making another decision: whether or not to enlist. Frost mailed 'The Road Not Taken' to Thomas, intending to amuse his friend with its satire. Irony apart, the poem reaches deep symbolic levels.

'Towards Chance's Pitch', Gilly Hancock

Putting in the Seed

You come to fetch me from my work to-night
When supper's on the table, and we'll see
If I can leave off burying the white
Soft petals fallen from the apple tree
(Soft petals, yes, but not so barren quite,
Mingled with these, smooth bean and wrinkled pea),
And go along with you ere you lose sight
Of what you came for and become like me,
Slave to a springtime passion for the earth.
How Love burns through the Putting in the Seed
On through the watching for that early birth
When, just as the soil tarnishes with weed,
The sturdy seedling with arched body comes
Shouldering its way and shedding the earth crumbs.

Robert Frost
(written at Little Iddens, 1914)

A Time to Talk

When a friend calls to me from the road
And slows his horse to a meaning walk,
I don't stand still and look around
On all the hills I haven't hoed,
And shout from where I am, "What is it?"
No, not as there is a time to talk.
I thrust my hoe in the mellow ground,
Blade-end up and five feet tall,
And plod: I go up to the stone wall
For a friendly visit.

Robert Frost
(written at Little Iddens, 1914)

Iris by night

One misty evening, one another's guide,
We two were groping down a Malvern side
The last wet fields and dripping hedges home.
There came a moment of confusing lights,
Such as according to belief in Rome
Were seen of old at Memphis on the heights
Before the fragments of a former sun
Could concentrate anew and rise as one.
Light was a paste of pigment in our eyes.
And then there was a moon and then a scene
So watery as to seem submarine;
In which we two stood saturated, drowned.
The clover-mingled rowan on the ground
Had taken all the water it could as dew,
And still the air was saturated too,
Its airy pressure turned to water weight.

Then a small rainbow like a trellis gate,
A very small moon-made prismatic bow,
Stood closely over us through which to go.
And then we were vouchsafed the miracle
That never yet to other two befell
And I alone of us have lived to tell.
A wonder! Bow and rainbow as it bent,
Instead of moving with us as we went
(To keep the pots of gold from being found),
It lifted from its dewy pediment
Its two mote-swimming many-colored ends
And gathered them together in a ring.
And we stood in it softly circled round
From all division time or foe can bring
In a relation of elected friends.

Robert Frost
(1936)

Frost addresses this poem to Edward Thomas. Frost remembers a moonbow that mysteriously encircled them on 'a Malvern side' in August 1914. On that day they had walked from Leddington to Bromsberrow, then through the Hollybush Gap to Castlemorton Common. They passed the reservoir, climbed to British Camp and descended the Ridgeway to Eastnor. The poem was published in 1936, but Frost probably wrote it eighteen years earlier.

48

The sun used to shine

The sun used to shine while we two walked
Slowly together, paused and started
Again, and sometimes mused, sometimes talked
As either pleased, and cheerfully parted

Each night. We never disagreed
Which gate to rest on. The to be
And the late past we gave small heed.
We turned from men or poetry

To rumours of the war remote
Only all both stood disinclined
For aught but the yellow flavorous coat
Of an apple wasps had undermined;

Or a sentry of dark betonies,
The stateliest of small flowers on earth,
At the forest verge; or crocuses
Pale purple as if they had their birth

In sunless Hades fields. The war
Came back to mind with the moonrise
Which soldiers in the east afar
Beheld then. Nevertheless, our eyes

Could as well imagine the Crusades
Or Caesar's battles. Everything
To faintness like those rumours fades –
Like the brook's water glittering

Under the moonlight – like those walks
Now – like us two that took them, and
The fallen apples, all the talks
And silences – like memory's sand

When the tide covers it late or soon,
And other men through other flowers
In those fields under the same moon
Go talking and have easy hours.

Edward Thomas
(1914)

49

Elizabeth's Song

Shining white clouds in the cherry trees tangled,
   And over the orchard snowing;
Silver wild cherries on the hill-side spangled,
   And bright among bronze oaks blowing:
So white, so bright, so fragrantly
Heart's delight blossoms in me.

Swallows come back to their endless careering
   In love and in finest feather;
Swerving down, close to the cowslips nearing,
   Then high in the golden weather:
In air so bright, with such a flight,
Dances on wings my heart's delight.

Lascelles Abercrombie

Follow my heart, my dancing feet

Two singing voices:

First Voice:

'Follow my heart, my dancing feet,
Dance as blithe as my heart can beat:
Dancing alone can understand
What a heavenly way we pass,
Treading the green and golden land,
Daffodillies and grass.'

Second Voice:

'I had a song, too, on my road,
But mine was in my eyes;
For Malvern Hills were with me all the way,
Singing loveliest visible melodies
Blue as a south-sea bay;
And ruddy as wine of France

Breadths of new-turn'd ploughland under them glowed.
'Twas my heart then must dance
To dwell in my delight;
No need to sing when all in song my sight
Moved over hills so musically made
And with such colour played. –
And only yesterday it was I saw
Veil'd in streamers of grey wavering smoke
My shapely Malvern Hills.
That was the last hail-storm to trouble spring:
He came in gloomy haste,
Pusht in front of the white clouds quietly basking,
In such a hurry he tript against the hills,
And stumbling forward spilt over his shoulders
All his black baggage held,
Streaking downpour of hail.
Then fled dismayed, and the sun in golden glee
And the high white clouds laught down his dusky ghost.'

Lascelles Abercrombie
from *Ryton Firs* (1919)

The Broken Gate

I know a little broken gate
   Beneath the apple-boughs and pines,
The seasons lend it coloured state,
   And round its hinge the ivy twines –
The ivy and the bloomless rose,
   And autumn berries flaming red;
The pine its gracious scent bestows,
   The apple-boughs their treasure shed.

It opens on an orchard hung
   With heavy-laden boughs that spill
Their brown and yellow fruit among
   The withered stems of daffodil:

The river from its shallows freed
   Here falls upon a stirless peace,
The tides of time suspended lead
   The tired spirit to release.

A little land of mellowed ease
   I find beyond my broken gate,
I hear amid the laden trees
   A magic song, and there elate
I pass along from sound and sight
   Of men who fret the world away, –
I gather rich and rare delight
   Where every day is holy day.

John Drinkwater

Daffodils

Again, my man of Lady Street,
Your daffodils have come, the sweet
Bell daffodils that are aglow
In Ryton woods now, where they go
Who are my friends and make good rhymes.

They come, these very daffodils,
From that same flight of Gloucester hills,
Where Dymock dames and Dymock men
Have cider kegs and flocks in pen,
For I've been there a thousand times.

Your petals are enchanted still
As when those tongues of Orphic skill
Bestowed upon that Ryton earth
A benediction for your birth,
Sun-daffodils that now I greet.

Because, brave daffodils, you bring
Colour and savour of a spring
That Ryton blood is quick to tell.
You should be borne, if all were well,
In golden carts to Lady Street.

John Drinkwater

53

This is the second poem which Drinkwater addressed to a greengrocer on Lady Street in Birmingham. 'My friends' who 'make good rhymes' refers to the other Dymock poets. Lascelles Abercrombie lived in Ryton at 'The Gallows'. He and the other poets praised the small daffodils that flower abundantly in Ryton.

A Sabbath Day in Five Watches

I. MORNING
(to M.C.)

You were three men and women two,
And well I loved you, all of you,
   And well we kept the Sabbath day.
The bells called out of Malvern town,
But never bell could call us down
   As we went up the hill away.

Was it a thousand years ago
Or yesterday that men were so
   Zealous of creed and argument?
Here wind is brother to the rain,
And the hills laugh upon the plain,
   And the old brain-gotten feuds are spent.

Bring lusty laughter, lusty jest,
Bring each the song he names the best,
   Bring eager thought and speech that's keen,
Tell each his tale and tell it out,
The only shame be prudent doubt,
   Bring bodies where the lust is clean.

IV. EVENSONG
(to B.M.)

Come, let us tell it over,
Each to each by the fireside,
How that earth has been a swift adventure for us,
And the watches of the day as a gay song and a right song,
And now the traveller wind has found a bed,
And the sheep crowd under the thorn.

      Good was the day and our travelling,
      And now there is evensong to sing.

Night, and along the valleys
Watch the eyes of the homesteads.
The dark hills are very still and still are the stars.
Patiently under the ploughlands the wheat moves and the
barley.
The secret hour of love is upon the sky,
And our thought in praise is aflame.

      Sing evensong as well we may
      For our travel upon this Sabbath day.

Earth, we have known you truly,
Heard your mutable music,
Have been your lovers and felt the savour of you,
And you have quickened in us the blood's fire and the heart's fire.
We have wooed and striven with you and made you ours
By the strength sprung out of your loins.

     Lift the latch on its twisted thong,
     And an end be made of our evensong.

John Drinkwater

'Malvern Priory in Winter', Gilly Hancock

Worcester Beacon

When every spur of whin's a spike of ice,
Each grassy tussock bristling blades of steel,
Each withered bracken-frond a rare device
Of sparkling crystal crackling under-heel
With brittle tinkling, then it is the time,
O Love, to leave the chilly hearth and climb
The sunlit Beacon, where the live airs blow
Along the clean wave-edge of drifted snow.

Love, let us go
And scale the ridge: I long to see you there
Breathing the eager air
With cheeks aglow,
The sunlight on your hair:
O Love, I long to share
With you a moment the white ecstasy
And crystal silence of eternity.

Wilfrid Gibson
(1921)

'Mist over the Malverns', Gilly Hancock

For G.

All night under the moon
Plovers are flying
Over the dreaming meadows of silvery light,
Over the meadows of June
Flying and crying –
Wandering voices of love in the hush of the night.

All night under the moon
Love, though we're lying
Quietly under the thatch, in the silvery light
Over the meadows of June
Together we're flying –
Rapturous voices of love in the hush of the night.

Wilfrid Gibson
(1916)

G. was Geraldine Townshend, whom Wilfrid married in December 1913. From the following February the two lived in the Old Nailshop at Greenway Cross.

The Ragged Stone

As I was walking with my dear, my dear come back at last,
The shadow of the Ragged Stone fell on us as we passed:

And if the tale be true they tell about the Ragged Stone,
I'll not be walking with my dear next year, nor yet alone.

And we're to wed come Michaelmas, my lovely dear and I;
And we're to have a little house, and do not want to die.

But all the folk are fighting in the lands across the sea,
Because the king and counsellors went mad in Germany.

Because the king and counsellors went mad, my love and I
May never have a little house before we come to die.

And if the tale be true they tell about the Ragged Stone
I'll not be walking with my dear next year, nor yet alone.

Wilfrid Gibson
(1920)

Legend tells that if the shadow of Ragged Stone Hill falls on a person, a death will follow. Ragged Stone Hill is south of Hollybush, north of White Leaved Oak.

The Golden Room (to G.)

Do you remember the still summer evening
When, in the cosy cream-washed living-room
Of the Old Nailshop, we all talked and laughed –
Our neighbours from The Gallows, Catherine
And Lascelles Abercrombie; Rupert Brooke;
Elinor and Robert Frost, living a while
At Little Iddens, who'd brought over with them
Helen and Edward Thomas? In the lamplight
We talked and laughed; but, for the most part, listened
While Robert Frost kept on and on and on,
In his slow New England fashion, for our delight,
Holding us with shrewd turns and racy quips,
And the rare twinkle of his grave blue eyes?

We sat there in the lamplight, while the day
Died from rose-latticed casements, and the plovers
Called over the low meadows, till the owls
Answered them from the elms; we sat and talked –
Now, a quick flash from Abercrombie; now,
A murmured dry half-heard aside from Thomas;
Now, a clear laughing word from Brooke; and then
Again Frost's rich and ripe philosophy
That had the body and tang of good draught-cider,
And poured as clear a stream.

     'Twas in July
Of nineteen-fourteen that we sat and talked:
Then August brought the war, and scattered us.

Now, on the crest of an Aegean isle
Brooke sleeps and dreams of England. Thomas lies
'Neath Vimy Ridge, where he, among his fellows,
Died, just as life had touched his lips to song.
And nigh as ruthlessly has life divided
Us who survive; for Abercrombie toils
In a black Northern town, beneath the glower
Of hanging smoke; and in America
Frost farms once more; and, far from the Old Nailshop,
We sojourn by the Western sea.

     And yet,
Was it for nothing that the little room
All golden in the lamplight, thrilled with golden
Laughter from hearts of friends that summer night?
Darkness has fallen on it, and the shadow
May never more be lifted from the hearts
That went through those black years of war, and live.

And still, whenever men and women gather
For talk and laughter on a summer night,
Shall not that lamp rekindle; and the room
Glow once again alive with light and laughter;
And, like a singing star in time's abyss,
Burn golden-hearted through oblivion?

Wilfrid Gibson (1925)

'Stack Building in the Malverns', Dame Laura Knight

In Flanders

I'm homesick for my hills again –
  My hills again!
To see above the Severn plain
Unscabbarded against the sky
The blue high blade of Cotswold lie;
The giant clouds go royally
By jagged Malvern with a train
Of shadows. Where the land is low
Like a huge imprisoning O
I hear a heart that's sound and high,
I hear the heart within me cry:
'I'm homesick for my hills again –
  My hills again!
Cotswold or Malvern, sun or rain!
  My hills again!'

F.W. Harvey

The Touchstone – Watching Malvern

What Malvern is the day is, and its touchstone –
Gray velvet, or moon-marked; rich, or bare as bone;
One looks towards Malvern and is made one with the whole;
The world swings round him as the Bear to the Pole.

Men have crossed seas to know how Paul's tops Fleet,
That as music has rapt them in the mere street,
While none or few care how the curved giants stand,
(Those upheaved strengths!) on the meadow and plough-land.

Ivor Gurney
(*c.*1920-3)

the Bear: the constellation Ursa Major
Paul's: St Paul's Cathedral
Fleet: Fleet Street (or perhaps the River Fleet which flows underneath London)

De Profundis

If only this fear would leave me I could dream of Crickley Hill
    And a hundred thousand thoughts of home would visit my heart in sleep;
But here the peace is shattered all day by the devil's will,
    And the guns bark night-long to spoil the velvet silence deep.

O who could think that once we drank in quiet inns and cool
    And saw brown oxen trooping the dry sands to slake
Their thirst at the river flowing, or plunged in a silver pool
    To shake the sleepy drowse off before well awake?

We are stale here, we are covered body and soul and mind
    With mire of the trenches, close clinging and foul,
We have left our old inheritance, our Paradise behind,
    And clarity is lost to us and cleanness of soul.

O blow here, you dusk-airs and breaths of half-light,
    And comfort despairs of your darlings that long
Night and day for sound of your bells, or a sight
    Of your tree-bordered lanes, land of blossom and song.

Autumn will be here soon, but the road of coloured leaves
         Is not for us, the up and down highway where go
Earth's pilgrims to wonder where Malvern upheaves
         That blue-emerald splendour under great clouds of snow.

Some day we'll fill in trenches, level the land and turn
         Once more joyful faces to the country where trees
Bear thickly for good drink, where strong sunsets burn
         Huge bonfires of glory – O God, send us peace!

Hard it is for men of moors or fens to endure
         Exile and hardship, or the northland grey-drear;
But we of the rich plain of sweet airs and pure,
         Oh! Death would take so much from us, how should we not fear?

Ivor Gurney
(1919)

Gurney had to write hurriedly in the trenches. In the fifth stanza, did he intend to write 'wander'? Or did he want to intrigue us with the double resonance of 'wonder' and 'wander'?

Larches

Larches are most fitting small red hills
That rise like swollen ant-heaps likeably
And modest before big things like near Malvern
Or Cotswold's further early Italian
Blue arrangement; unassuming as the
Cowslips, celandines, buglewort and daisies
That trinket out the green swerves like a child's game.
O never so careless or lavish as here.
I thought, 'You beauty! I must rise soon one dawn time
And ride to see the first beam strike on you
Of gold or ruddy recognisance over
Crickley level or Bredon sloping down.
I must play tunes like Burns, or sing like David,
A saying out of what the hill leaves unexprest;
The tale or song that lives in it, and is sole,
A round red thing, green upright things of flame.'
It is May, and the conceited cuckoo toots and whoos his name.

Ivor Gurney

Ivor Gurney cycled to The Gallows in Ryton in April 1916. Larches flourish in Ryton Firs and on 'the small red hills' of neighbouring Redmarley. In a letter Gurney described Redmarley: 'that little village set under the shadow of the Malverns and set with orchards thick and fair with blossom and flowers. Cowslips, daffodils, bluebells, ladysmocks; all Shakespearean like the country – a perfect setting for the old comedy.' (Gurney's final reference is to A Midsummer Night's Dream.*)*

'Landscape of the Malvern Distance', Paul Nash

A Summer Night (to Geoffrey Hoyland)

W.H. Auden liked to sleep under the stars. The dedication of A Summer Night *is to the headmaster of the Downs School, Colwall, where Auden was teaching. Auden expected a European calamity as devastating as a tsunami. The inner peacefulness of the pre-war evening would, he believed, assuage violence and inspire later reconstruction. Auden once related that he experienced a 'vision of* agape*', an awareness of universal goodness and love, on Hoyland's lawn in Colwall. In* A Summer Night *he alludes to this.*

'One fine summer night in June 1933 I was sitting on a lawn after dinner with three colleagues, two women and one man. We liked each other well enough but we were certainly not intimate friends, nor had any one of us a sexual interest in another. Incidentally, we had not drunk any alcohol. We were talking casually about everyday matters when, quite suddenly and unexpectedly, something happened. I felt myself invaded by a power which, though I consented to it, was irresistible and certainly not mine. For the first time in my life I knew exactly – because, thanks to the power, I was doing it – what it means to love one's neighbour as oneself. I was also certain, though the conversation continued to be perfectly ordinary, that my three colleagues were having the same experience. (In the case of one of them, I was later able to confirm this.) My personal feelings towards them were unchanged – they were still colleagues, not intimate friends – but I felt their existence as themselves to be of infinite value and rejoiced in it ...

The experience lasted at its full intensity for about two hours when we said good-night to each other and went to bed. When I awoke the next morning, it was still present, though weaker, and it did not vanish completely for two days or so. The memory of the experience has not prevented me making use of others, grossly and often, but it has made it much more difficult for me to deceive myself about what I am up to when I do. And among the various factors which several years later brought me back to the Christian faith in which I had been brought up, the memory of this experience and asking myself what it could mean was one of the most crucial, though, at the time it occurred, I thought I had done with Christianity for good.'

A Summer Night (to Geoffrey Hoyland)

Out on the lawn I lie in bed,
Vega conspicuous overhead
   In the windless nights of June,
As congregated leaves complete
Their day's activity; my feet
   Point to the rising moon.

Lucky, this point in time and space
Is chosen as my working-place,
   Where the sexy airs of summer,
The bathing hours and the bare arms,
The leisured drives through a land of farms
   Are good to a newcomer.

Equal with colleagues in a ring
I sit on each calm evening
   Enchanted as the flowers
The opening light draws out of hiding
With all its gradual dove-like pleading,
   Its logic and its powers:

That later we, though parted then,
May still recall these evenings when
   Fear gave his watch no look;
The lion griefs loped from the shade
And on our knees their muzzles laid,
   And Death put down his book.

Now north and south and east and west
Those I love lie down to rest;
   The moon looks on them all,
The healers and the brilliant talkers,
The eccentrics and the silent walkers,
   The dumpy and the tall.

She climbs the European sky,
Churches and power-stations lie
   Alike among earth's fixtures:
Into the galleries she peers
And blankly as a butcher stares
   Upon the marvellous pictures.

To gravity attentive, she
Can notice nothing here, though we
 Whom hunger does not move,
From gardens where we feel secure
Look up and with a sigh endure
 The tyrannies of love:

And, gentle, do not care to know,
Where Poland draws her eastern bow,
 What violence is done,
Nor ask what doubtful act allows
Our freedom in this English house,
 Our picnics in the sun.

Soon, soon, through dykes of our content
The crumpling flood will force a rent
 And, taller than a tree,
Hold sudden death before our eyes
Whose river dreams long hid the size
 And vigours of the sea.

But when the waters make retreat
And through the black mud first the wheat
 In shy green stalks appears,
When stranded monsters gasping lie,
And sounds of riveting terrify
 Their whorled unsubtle ears,

May these delights we dread to lose,
This privacy, need no excuse
 But to that strength belong,
As through a child's rash happy cries
The drowned parental voices rise
 In unlamenting song.

After discharges of alarm
All unpredicted let them calm
 The pulse of nervous nations,
Forgive the murderer in his glass,
Tough in their patience to surpass
 The tigress her swift motions.

W.H. Auden
(1933)

'Colwall Oaks', H.H. Lines

Here on the cropped grass of the narrow ridge I stand

Here on the cropped grass of the narrow ridge I stand.
A fathom of earth, alive in air,
Aloof as an admiral on the old rocks,
   England below me:
Eastward across the Midland plains
An express is leaving for a sailor's country;
   Westward is Wales
Where on clear evenings the retired and rich
From the french windows of their sheltered mansions
See the Sugarloaf standing, an upright sentinel
   Over Abergavenny.

When last I stood here I was not alone; happy
Each thought the other, thinking of a crime,
And England to our meditations seemed
   The perfect setting:
But now it has no innocence at all ...

W.H. Auden
from *Malvern* (1936)

'Worcestershire Beacon', Gilly Hancock

Edward Elgar 1857-1934

1

A boy among the reeds on Severn shore
Sound-bathing: a ghost humming his 'cello tune
Upon the Malvern hills: and in between,
Mostly enigma. Who shall read this score?

The stiff, shy, blinking man in a norfolk suit:
The martinet: the gentle-minded squire:
The piano-tuner's son from Worcestershire:
The Edwardian grandee: how did they consort

In such luxuriant themes? Not privilege
Nor talent's cute, obsequious ear attuned
His soul to the striding rhythms, the unimpugned
Melancholy of a vulgar, vivid age.

Genius alone can move by singular ways
Yet home to the heart of all, the common chord;
Beat to its own time, timelessly make heard
A long-breathed statement or a hesitant phrase.

For me, beyond the marches of his pride,
Through the dark airs and rose-imperial themes,
A far West-country summer glares and glooms,
A boy calls from the reeds on Severn side.

2

Orchards are in it – the vale of Evesham blooming:
Rainshine of orchards blowing out of the past.
The sadness of remembering orchards that never bore,
Never for us bore fruit: year after year they fruited,
But all, all was premature –
We were not ripe to gather the full beauty.
And now when I hear 'orchards' I think of loss, recall
White tears of blossom streaming away downwind
And wish the flower could have stayed to be one
  with the fruit it formed.
Oh, coolness at the core of early summers,
Woodwind haunting those green expectant alleys,
Our blossom falling, falling.

Hills are in it – the Malverns, Bredon, Cotswold.
A meadowsweetness of high summer days:
Clovering bees, time-honeyed bells, the lark's top C.
Hills where each sound, like larksong, passes into light,
And light is music all but seen.
Dawn's silvery tone and evening's crimson adagio;
Noonday on the full strings of sunshine simmering, dreaming,
No past, no future, the pulse of time unnoticed:
Cloud-shadows sweeping in arpeggios up the hillsides;

Grey, muted light which, brooding on stone, tree, clover
And cornfield, makes their colours sing most clear –
All moods and themes of light.

And a river – call it the Severn – a flowing-awayness.
Bray of moonlight on water; brassy flamelets
Of marigold, buttercup, flag-iris in water-meadows;
Kingfishers, mayflies, mills, regattas: the ever-rolling
Controlled percussion of thunderous weirs.
Rivers are passionate gods: they flood, they drown,
Roar themselves hoarse, ripple to gaiety, lull the land
With slow movements of tender meditation.
And in it too, in his music, I hear the famous river –
Always and never the same, carrying far
Beyond our view, reach after noble reach –
That bears its sons away.

Cecil Day-Lewis

Part of 'Severn above Worcester', H.H. Lines

Mid June on Chase End Hill

There are explosions on umbrella'd leaves
wet rain on warm earth.
Powerful rays spotlight my path
And I am washed by wet leaves as I pass.

A smell of green freshness permeates skin,
I breathe deeply,
then hear it, a beautiful hymn from
a thrush's notes, in triple calls,
practising scales as rain still falls.
Up up he goes to glorious heights,
thrilling air with purest sound,
while far below, on muddy ground,
trees stand, rustling jubilation.

Jane Amherst

September Chase End Hill

After summer, plaintiveness descends.
Rain-drenched elderberries hang limp,
ferns bend in obeisance to water,
nettles, bright green, shimmer.
Nature no longer droops in heat
but a wet coldness beats a different rhythm,
A slow, ageing, rheumatic tread.

Leaves fall in dead curls,
swirled patterns of confusion,
hiding muddied paths where horses tread,
and hints of foxes, mice and life.

Pheasants wait for they know not what,
sensing danger soon to come,
watching carefully human approach,
crouching down in tall bracken,

a restless need to take flight stirring,
until with squawks, flutters, whirring,
they startle and fly, scuttle in protest,
alarming everything within a mile and a half.

I laugh as I watch them,
the late sun making their plumage glow,
the damp air carrying mist to muffle
their squawks, croaks, gossipy warnings.

Cobwebs cling, gnats dance,
evening shadows lull my soul
as I head for home,
treading a wine press of fallen plums.

Jane Amherst

The Gullet in Winter – November 25th

It's cold! Fingers are clumsy, feet are stone.
I am alone, above the quarry.
Here there is light,
but below shadows tumble
fingering pillars of rock, catching crags,
sliding, diving to deep water.
The quarry sinks in sullen silence down,
down through icy water
surrendering to mysterious darkness.
Only the surface gives hope
in its reflection of blue sky.

Jane Amherst

The lives of the poets

WILLIAM LANGLAND (1330?-1386?) may once have been a monk at Malvern Priory, or at Little Malvern; verses in *Piers Plowman* reveal that its author knew the Malvern Hills. He served in minor orders in London. Langland's name (and the different name of his father) we learn from a memorandum on a 15th-century manuscript of *Piers Plowman*, now in Trinity College, Dublin: 'Stacy de Rokayle was the father of William de Langland; this Stacy was of gentle birth and lived in Shipton-under-Wychwood, a tenant of Lord Spenser in the County of Oxfordshire. The aforesaid William made the book which is called *Piers Plowman*.'

MICHAEL DRAYTON (1563-1631), born in Warwickshire, moved to London, where he was among the friends of Ben Jonson and of the antiquaries John Stowe and William Camden. He wrote odes, eclogues, satires, sonnets and historical poems.

JOHN DYER (1699-1757) was student at Westminster School, lawyer in Wales, artist in Italy, farmer near Bromyard in Herefordshire and near Nuneaton, and Rector of parishes in Leicestershire and Lincolnshire. Throughout he wrote poetry. His poem *Grongar Hill* describes his homeland in the Vale of the Towy. *The Fleece*, a long georgic, celebrates wise shepherding and explains spinning, weaving, dyeing and the world-wide wool-trade.

ROBERT BLOOMFIELD (1766-1823), Suffolk born, worked on a farm from the age of twelve. Insufficiently robust, he went to London as a cobbler. Besides making shoes, Bloomfield fashioned aeolian harps and wrote poetry. *The Farmer's Boy* (1800) – 1,500 lines of heroic couplets – won him society's attention, Southey's and Wordsworth's admiration, and some relief from poverty. In 1807, with Thomas Baker of Stroud and other friends from Gloucestershire, he boated down the Wye. Reduced to penury once more by the fraud of a publisher, he moved his family to Bedfordshire.

WILLIAM LISLE BOWLES (1762-1850) was educated at Winchester and Trinity College, Oxford. Thwarted love tinges his early poems; Byron was to call him 'the maudlin prince of mournful sonnet-eers'. Robert Southey and S.T. Coleridge thought otherwise. They admired Bowles' *Sonnets Written Chiefly on Picturesque Spots during a Journey* (1789), and to him in 1796 Coleridge dedicated his *Poems*. Bowles married, became a clergyman, magistrate and antiquary, Rector of Dumbleton in Gloucestershire in 1797, Vicar of Bremhill in Wiltshire in 1804, Chaplain to the Prince Regent in 1818 and Canon Residentiary at Salisbury Cathedral in 1828.

JOSEPH COTTLE (1770-1853) was a Bristol bookseller, publisher and author. He helped to finance Coleridge and Southey when they planned to found a Pantisocracy, abetted their courtship of the Fricker sisters, and commissioned their portraits. Cottle published Southey's poems, and also published the *Lyrical Ballads* of Wordsworth and Coleridge in 1798, in which year he produced *Malvern Hills*. Cottle, a bachelor, was a devout dissenter, and was keen to improve the lot of the poor.

JAMES BISSET (1762?-1832), born in Perth, served as artist's apprentice in Birmingham. He devised a way in which he could paint on the inside of a glass, establishing his own business. He also worked as a coiner and maker of celebratory medallions. Bisset joined the Minerva Club, a group which met at Birmingham's Leicester Arms to discuss politics. His topical verse appeared often in the *Gentleman's Magazine*. Bisset lived in Leamington from 1813 and wrote *A Picturesque Guide to Leamington*.

WILLIAM WORDSWORTH (1770-1850), Poet Laureate from 1843, was born in Cockermouth, schooled in Hawkshead, and attended St John's College, Cambridge. With Dorothy his sister he lived for two years on the Quantock Hills, close to Samuel Taylor Coleridge. Their *Lyrical Ballads* were published in 1798. After that the Wordsworths – William, Dorothy and Mary (née Hutchinson), whom William married – lived in or near Grasmere in Cumbria, first at Dove Cottage, later at Rydal Mount. Mary's relations at times had homes in Radnorshire, Herefordshire and Malvern.

HENRY ALFORD (1810-71) was President of the Cambridge Union. At Trinity College he was close to both Alfred Tennyson and Arthur Hallam. Poet, composer and painter, from 1857 he was Dean of Canterbury. Alford composed hymns still widely known: 'Come ye thankful people, come' and 'Ten thousand times ten thousand'. His edited text of the *New Testament* has been a standard for biblical theologians. *Poems and Poetical Fragments* was published in 1831, other poems, including his verse translation of *The Odyssey*, later. He married most happily his cousin Fanny on 10th March, 1835, to which event he refers in his sonnet *Malvern Hill*.

THOMAS BABINGTON MACAULAY (1800-59) wrote for *The Edinburgh Review*, was a member of the Supreme Council of India, was elected MP and served as Secretary at War and Paymaster General. His popular four-volume *History of England* was well-researched, a proud Whig defence of the English constitution. Macaulay's rollicking *Lays of Ancient Rome*, to which were appended *The Armada* and other poems about English events, appeared in 1842. He was raised to the peerage as Lord Macaulay in 1857.

ELIZABETH BARRETT (BROWNING) (1806-61) was largely self-educated at Hope End, on the western border of Colwall. Precocious and intellectually disciplined, she corresponded with literary neighbours, including Uvedale Price. Her poem, *The Battle of Marathon*, was published when she was fourteen years old. EBB loved the landscape of the Malvern Hills, from which she was separated when she was 26, her family moving to Sidmouth and then to London. Despite being reclusive, she exchanged letters with Robert Browning, to whom she was secretly married in 1846. The two left for Italy; Casa Guidi in Florence became the Brownings' home. EBB's *Sonnets from the Portuguese* appeared in 1850; *Aurora Leigh* in 1857.

JOHN ADDINGTON SYMONDS (1840-93), son of a Bristol physician, was a pupil of Benjamin Jowett at Balliol College, Oxford. He won the Newdigate prize for poetry and was to write several volumes of verse. Lean and handsome as a young man, he was stressed by love repressed and by the tubercular consumption that was to shorten his life. Symonds married and had four daughters to whom he remained close, but came to acknowledge his homosexuality. In *Studies of the Greek Poets* and *A Problem of Greek Ethics* he celebrated Platonic love, and later he co-authored with Havelock Ellis pioneering works of sexual liberation. At Davos in Switzerland and at Venice he entertained a wide circle of literary guests. Several of Symonds' works are accepted as classics: *The Renaissance in Italy* (in many volumes) and his translations of *The Sonnets of Michelangelo Buonarroti* and *The Life of Benvenuto Cellini*.

ALFRED EDWARD HOUSMAN (1859-1936) went to Bromsgrove School and St John's College, Oxford, where, to general astonishment, he failed finals. He became a clerk in the Patent Office, in the evenings studying in the British Museum Library and producing papers on the texts of Greek and Latin authors. In 1892 he became Professor of Latin at University College, London, and in 1892 Professor at Cambridge, where he lived in Trinity College. *The Shropshire Lad*, 63 lyrics, was published in 1896 and quietly received. Its themes of nature, love, war and death won the book popularity twenty years later. *Last Poems* (1922) and *More Poems* (1936) followed.

JOHN MASEFIELD (1878-1967), Ledbury born, went to Warwick School, then, in 1891, to the training-ship *HMS Conway*. In 1894 he sailed for Chile round the Horn, and to New York, where he jumped ship. Masefield's enthusiasm for tall ships, and for the traditions, language and shanties of those who sailed them, abided. *Salt-water Ballads* was published in 1902. The ruffian society of Ledbury was the scene of his long poem *The Everlasting Mercy* (1911). *Reynard the Fox* celebrated rural life and its pathos. In 1930 Masefield became Poet Laureate. He lived on Boars Hill, outside Oxford.

MARGUERITE RADCLYFFE HALL (1883-1943) assumed male attire and liked to be called John or Radclyffe. Her *Songs of Three Counties* were published, with other volumes of lyrics, between 1906 and 1915. Radclyffe Hall's novel *The Well of Loneliness* (1928) was banned in England, but republished in 1949, and remains a lesbian classic. It was the fifth of seven novels of psychological insight, preceded by *Adam's Breed*, a best-seller and winner of literary prizes.

ROBERT FROST (1874-1963) grew up in New England, where he taught in colleges, farmed, and wrote for a poultry magazine. In 1912 he sailed to England with his wife and family. The Frosts lived at Little Iddens in Leddington (within the parish of Dymock) enjoying the friendship of Abercrombie and Gibson and the visits of Edward Thomas. Frost's first collection of poems, *A Boy's Will*, was published in 1913, to be followed by *North of Boston* (1914). Robert Frost remains one of the most popular American poets.

EDWARD THOMAS (1878-1917) attended Lincoln College, Oxford, married Helen while a student, reviewed poetry, and wrote biographies and topographical works. In Leddington, Robert Frost encouraged him to write poetry. Edward Thomas enlisted in 1915 and was killed in the battle of Arras.

LASCELLES ABERCROMBIE (1882-1938) attended Malvern College and Owen's College, Manchester. In Liverpool he wrote reviews for papers and engaged with the city's cultural life. In 1910, Lascelles and his wife Catherine, an artist, moved first to Much Marcle, and then to The Gallows at Ryton. The quarterly *New Numbers* contained Abercrombie's poems and those of John Drinkwater, Wilfrid Gibson and Rupert Brooke, and was mainly edited by Abercrombie. The Gallows became a venue for poets – John Haines and Ivor Gurney, as well as those living in Greenway and Leddington. Rupert Brooke loved that house 'where one drinks great mugs of cider, & looks at fields of poppies'. After the war Abercrombie was Professor of English at Liverpool and Leeds universities, and finally Fellow of Merton College, Oxford.

JOHN DRINKWATER (1882-1937) left Oxford High School at fifteen. He spent thirteen years in insurance before joining Barry Jackson to establish the Pilgrim Players in Birmingham (later the Birmingham Repertory Theatre). Drinkwater was actor, theatre administrator, playwright and poet. His plays included *Abraham Lincoln*, a success in both London and New York. He became a friend of Rupert Brooke and, contributing to *New Numbers*, frequently visited Dymock.

WILFRID GIBSON (1878-1962) was born in Hexham. His tough early poems were hailed as the voice of the Northumberland common man. In 1912 Gibson moved to London where he lodged above the Poetry Bookshop and entered the circle of Eddie Marsh, editor of Georgian Poetry. When he married Geraldine the pair took The Old Nailshop at Greenway Cross. Gibson in his turn urged Robert Frost to move to the neighbourhood.

F.W. HARVEY (FREDERICK WILLIAM) (1888-1957) grew up in Minsterworth. At Kings School, Gloucester he became a friend of Ivor Gurney. Later, he practised as a solicitor in Gloucester and in the Forest of Dean. When war broke out in 1914 Harvey and his brothers enlisted in the Gloucester regiment. For bravery amidst trench warfare he was awarded the Distinguished Conduct Medal. Commissioned in 1916, Harvey soon after was captured. The poems he wrote at the Front and in German prison camp were his finest. Harvey's talks on the radio in his last years were popular; often they told about life in the Forest of Dean.

Ivor Gurney (1890-1937) was for six years boy-chorister at Gloucester Cathedral, a friend of F.W. Harvey and of Herbert Howells. He won a scholarship to the Royal School of Music, where his brilliance and instability were evident. In 1915 he enlisted in the 2/5th Glosters and was sent to France as a private. In the trenches he wrote poems and songs. Wounded, gassed, shell-shocked, in 1917 Gurney was invalided to Edinburgh. His music was published and performed. He was declared insane and spent the last fifteen years of his life in asylums, still composing, still writing, unable to visit the 'Severn meadows' which he loved passionately.

W.H. Auden (Wystan Hugh) (1907-73), a poet of outstanding stature, taught for three years (1932-1935) and for one term later, at the Downs School in Colwall. His first collection, *Poems 1930*, had already been published. While at the Downs he worked on his play *The Dog Beneath the Skin* and wrote brilliant poems. In Colwall, on a lawn sitting with others in a circle, he experienced a vision of *agape* – of pervading love – which, he later said, influenced his return to Christianity. In 1938 Auden visited the USA with Christopher Isherwood, and stayed. He became an American citizen, but often visited Oxford, where his old college, Christ Church, allowed him a cottage. He lived also in Austria.

CECIL DAY-LEWIS (1904-72) jointly edited *Oxford Poetry 1926*. At Oxford, Day-Lewis associated with W.H. Auden, Louis MacNeice and Stephen Spender, whose poetry shared with his a socialist critique of society. From 1930 to 1935 Day-Lewis, married with two sons, taught at Cheltenham junior school. Under the pseudonym Nicholas Blake he wrote twenty detective novels; their success enabled a move to east Devon, close to Hardy country. There his poetry became rural and personal, his voice authentically his own. Day-Lewis translated Virgil's *Georgics, Aeneid* and *Eclogues,* became friends with Rosamond Lehmann, and in 1949 married the 24-year-old actress Jill Balcon (their son is the actor Daniel Day-Lewis). Together they promoted public poetry readings. Day-Lewis was created Poet Laureate in 1968.

JANE AMHERST (1951-), born in Cheltenham, studied at the Rose Bruford College of Speech and Drama. From Tewkesbury, Jane moved to Birtsmorton at the foot of the Malverns, where for three years she rose early to walk with her dog on the hills. It was then that she began writing seriously. Now in Ledbury, Jane enjoys painting, contemplative walks, gardening, and visiting three grandchildren.

The lives of the artists

J.M.W. TURNER (JOSEPH MALLORD WILLIAM) (1775-1851), water-colourist and painter in oils, travelled below the Malverns when eighteen years of age. Prodigious talent had been recognised in him; for a couple of years he had exhibited at the Royal Academy. In 1793 he was returning from a visit to Wales and the Marches, the beginning of his routine: summers touring and sketching, winters painting in a London studio. Enthusiastic in observation of nature, Turner deployed remarkable visual memory and effortless draftsmanship. His small bound sketchbooks – 282 are in the Tate Gallery – trained his eye and informed larger compositions. John Ruskin was to hail Turner as the artist who could most 'stirringly and truthfully measure the moods of nature . . .the greatest of the age'. Turner's paintings of shimmering climatic effects and of pure, evanescent light still win admiration.

HENRY HARRIS LINES (1800-89) was the eldest son, amongst several artistic siblings, of Birmingham painter Samuel Lines. From the age of eighteen he exhibited at the Royal Academy and in Birmingham. His paintings were of landscapes or ancient buildings in the Midlands, Switzerland, North Yorkshire and north Wales. Worcester was his home from 1832. A keen archaeologist in his later years, Lines depicted sites with draftsman's skill. *The Ancient Camps on the Malvern Hills* was published posthumously in 1891.

PAUL NASH (1889-1946), a leading modernist, stayed at Madams in Upleadon in the 1940s. Ailing then, he painted the distant Malverns from that house and from Cleeve Hill near Cheltenham. Nash was predominately a landscape artist. Poetic and dreamlike images of southern England rendered in cool and delicate colours were often touched by Cubism and Surrealism. A pillar, a fallen tree-trunk, a wrecked aeroplane might be in mysterious juxtaposition to a rural vista. Hauntingly iconic are his First World War paintings of no-man's-land, a chaos of cratered earth and blasted trees. By simplification Nash sought to elicit the *genius loci* of a setting.

DAME LAURA KNIGHT (1877-1970), born Laura Johnson, was taught by her mother to draw, and entered Nottingham School of Art at fourteen. There she met Harold Knight; they married a dozen years later. In 1907 they moved to Newlyn in Cornwall, where artists had gathered around Stanhope Forbes and Elizabeth Armstrong. Laura painted out of doors, and her canvases capture the Cornish light, sea and sunshine, bodies of bathers and wind-swirled dresses, cliff-top picnics, and fishermen and women at their nets. Sir Barry Jackson, founder of Birmingham Rep, met the Knights in 1914 and arranged for Laura to paint Diaghelev's ballet behind the scenes. Later she studied circus performers, gypsies and hop-pickers. Through the 1930s Barry Jackson invited Dame Laura (as she was by then) and Harold to lively parties at Blackhill East to celebrate the Malvern festivals which he had initiated. The Knights enjoyed rambling in the hills and, caught by the outbreak of war, remained in the Malverns, settling first at the British Camp Hotel (now the Malvern Hills Hotel). Their studio was in the former stable at Windsacre, home of Allardyce Nicol, which looked westward over Herefordshire.

Laura's landscapes of her late Malvern period are among her best. She said: 'What entranced me most were the immense views so detailed with patchwork, with little shapes of fields and red-roofed farms, cattle in the fields, and hens pecking around the farmyards; it was all so enormous and filled with details. I loved it because no one else had painted it. But it is difficult when you are used to the ordinary thing to become accustomed to anything so great; it took years before I could ever attempt it all.' In old age she said: 'I long for another glimpse of the top of the Beacon, of the sparkle of the Bristol Channel at midday. I long again to hold a sketch-book and note down the ever-changing effects made by the weather on those open stretches of English country. And perhaps above all I long to spend many hours with the many dear friends Harold and I had the good fortune to make amidst that great beauty.'

GILLY HANCOCK. Born in Leeds, Gilly spent her early years near Malvern. She studied painting and ceramics at Cheltenham Teacher Training College, has lived in Colwall since her marriage, and for seventeen years taught at the Downs School. She is now able to pursue her love of painting in oils, inspired by the Malvern Hills which provide ever-changing scenes throughout the year. You can make an appointment to visit her studio in Colwall – gilly.h@btconnect.com.

MONTGOMERY SHREWSBURY COALBROOK·DALE SHIFFNAL

THE WREKIN WELLINGTON BRIDGNORTH

BISHOPS CASTLE CHURCH STRETTON MUCH WENLOCK

CRAVEN ARMS

KNIGHTON LUDLOW GLEE HILL ABBERLEY HILLS

WOOFERTON TENBURY WITLEY PARK

LEOMINSTER

NORTH HILL

CASTLE FROMA

BROMYARD

CRADLEY RIFLE BUTTS

MATHON

SUGAR LOAF HILL

WEST MALVERN

BEACON

HENRY GUY, LITH, MALVERN

MALVERN:— VIEW FROM THE WO

WOLVERHAMPTON   BILSTON   DUDLEY   WEST BROMWICH   BIRMINGHAM   LEAMINGTON WARWICK

BEWDLEY   KIDDERMINSTER   STOURBRIDGE   BROOMSGROVE   STRAFFORD-on-AVON

STOURPORT   HARTLEBURY JUNCTION   DROITWICH   EVESHAM

PERSHORE

WORCESTER   SPETCHLEY

HENWICK   KEMPSEY   CROOME PARK

RIVER TEME   RIVER SEVERN

BRANSFORD   POWICK   COUNTY ASYLUM   OLD HILLS

MADRESFIELD COURT

NEWLAND

NORTH MALVERN

COWLEIGH

MALVERN LINK   STATION

ST ANNS WELL

HOLY MOUNT

ASSEMBLY ROOMS

PUBLISHED BY H. GUY, MALVERN.

ERSHIRE BEACON LOOKING NORTH

Index of sources

Abercrombie, Lascelles, *Poems* (OUP, 1930)

Alford, Henry, *Poetical Works* (Rivingtons, 1859)

Amherst, Jane © the author

Auden, W.H., *Look, Stranger!* (Faber, 1936)

Bisset, James, verse kindly offered to the editor in MSS by Roy
  Palmer of Malvern, folklorist and historian of folk songs

Bloomfield, Robert, *The Banks of Wye: a Poem in Four Books*
  (London, 1811, 1813, 1823)

Bowles, William Lisle, *Fourteen Sonnets, Elegiac and Descriptive,
  written during a Tour* (1789)

Browning, Elizabeth Barrett, *Poetical Works in Six Volumes* (Smith,
  Elder & Co., 1890)

Cottle, Joseph, *Malvern Hills: a poem* (T.M. Longman, 1798)

Day-Lewis, Cecil, *Complete Poems* (Stanford University Press, 1992)

Drayton, Michael, *Complete Works*, ed. Richard Hosper
  (John Russell Smith, London 1876)

Drinkwater, John, *Collected Poems* (Sidgwick and Jackson, 1923)

Dyer, John, *Poems* (J. Dodsley, in Pall-mall, 1770)

Frost, Robert, *Poetry*, ed. E.C. Lathem (Jonathan Cape, 1976)

Gibson, Wilfrid, *Collected Poems 1905-1925* (Macmillan, 1926)

Gurney, Ivor, *Collected Poems*, ed. P.J. Kavanagh (Fyfield Books/
  Carcanet, 2004)

Harvey, F.W., *Selected Poems of F.W. Harvey*, ed. Anthony Boden
  and R.K.R. Thornton (Douglas McLean, 2011)

Housman, A.E., *A Shropshire Lad* (George G. Harrap, 1940)

Langland, William, *The Vision of Piers Plowman*, ed. A.V.C.
  Schmidt (Everyman, J.M. Dent, 1995)

Macaulay, Thomas Babington, *Lays of Ancient Rome* (1842)

Masefield, John, *Collected Poems* (Heinemann, 1932)

Radclyffe Hall, Marguerite, *Songs of Three Counties and other
  poems* (Ferrero Press, 2013)

Symonds, John Addington, *New and Old: A Volume of Verse* (1880)

Thomas, Edward, *Collected Poems,* ed. R. George Thomas
  (Faber, 2004)

Wordsworth, William, *Poetical Works*, ed. Thomas Hutchinson
  (OUP, 1916)

Publisher's acknowledgements

Many thanks to John Croft and the Estate of Dame Laura Knight DBE RA 2014 for their kind permission to reproduce six of her paintings, and to the following institutions for supplying the images: 'Stack Building, Malvern Hills' (Bridgeman Art Library); 'The Malvern Hills' (Bridgeman Art Library); 'Changing Weather' (Government Art Collection, UK); 'The Plough' (Bridgeman Art Library); 'Harvest' (Art Gallery of South Australia) and 'Sundown' (Wolverhampton Art Gallery).

Thanks as well to Philippa Tinsley, Curator of Worcester City Art Gallery, who kindly made available H.H. Lines' painting 'The British Camp and Herefordshire Beacon', and to the Tate Gallery for permission to include 'Landscape of the Malvern Distance' by Paul Nash (supplied by Bridgeman Art Library) and J.M.W. Turner's sketch 'View of the Herefordshire Beacon, or British Camp, near Malvern'. We are also grateful to be able to include three drawings by H.H. Lines: 'Colwall Oaks' and 'Severn above Worcester', which are from the collection of the Royal Birmingham Society of Artists, and 'British Camp', which is dated 1860 and held by the Society of Antiquaries of London.

Thank you to the Malvern Conservators for the image of Great Malvern on the contents page and to Pat Palmer for photographing it, and to Pat Welch for allowing us to photograph the lithograph by Henry Guy of Malvern showing north and south views of Malvern from the Worcestershire Beacon.

Every effort has been made to trace copyright holders of the poems included in this anthology. Our grateful thanks go to Curtis Brown, New York for permission to quote W.H. Auden; to Random House for permission to quote Robert Frost; to Pan Macmillan for permission to quote Wilfrid Wilson Gibson; to Mrs Marie Griffiths and the F.W. Harvey Society for permission to quote F.W. Harvey; to Fraser, Peters & Dunlop for permission to quote Cecil Day-Lewis; and to the Society of Authors for permission to quote John Masefield.

Many thanks also to the National Portrait Gallery, which provided almost all of the images of the poets and artists.

94

'British Camp', H.H. Lines